W9-CRZ-544

Senses in My World

Hearing

by Martha E. H. Rustad

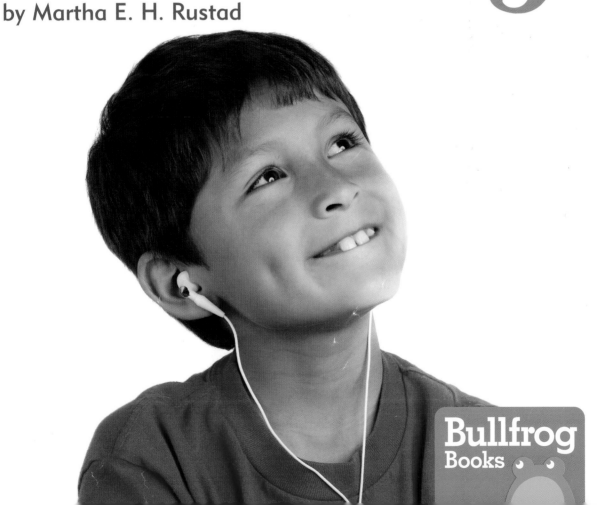

Bullfrog Books

Ideas for Parents and Teachers

Bullfrog Books let children practice reading informational text at the earliest reading levels. Repetition, familiar words, and photo labels support early readers.

Before Reading

- Ask the child to think about senses. Ask: How do you hear?

- Look at the picture glossary together. Read and discuss the words.

Read the Book

- "Walk" through the book and look at the photos. Let the child ask questions. Point out the photo labels.

- Read the book to the child, or have him or her read independently.

After Reading

- Prompt the child to think more. Ask: What sounds do you hear? How do sounds help you learn things?

Bullfrog Books are published by Jump!
5357 Penn Avenue South
Minneapolis, MN 55419
www.jumplibrary.com

Library of Congress Cataloging-in-Publication Data

Rustad, Martha E. H. (Martha Elizabeth Hillman), 1975-
  Hearing / by Martha E.H. Rustad.
    pages cm. — (Senses in my world)
  Audience: Age 5-8.
  Audience: K to grade 3.
  Includes bibliographical references and index.
  Summary: "This photo-illustrated book for young readers describes how hearing works and what we learn about our surroundings through our sense of hearing" — Provided by publisher.
  ISBN 978-1-62031-115-8 (hard cover) —
  ISBN 978-1-62496-182-3 (ebook) —
  ISBN 978-1-62031-149-3 (paperback)
  1. Hearing — Juvenile literature.
  2. Ear — Juvenile literature. I. Title.
  QP462.2.R87 2015
  612.8'5—dc23
                                    2013047821

Series Editor: Rebecca Glaser
Series Designer: Ellen Huber
Book Designer: Anna Peterson
Photo Researcher: Kurtis Kinneman

Photo Credits: All photos by Shutterstock except: Dreamstime/Alexey Arkhipov, 8, 23tl; Dreamstime/Oksix, 18 inset, 23tr; Getty Images/ BLOOMimage, 14–15; iStock/diego _ cervo, 9; iStock/monkeybusinessimages, 12–13; iStock/ srugina, 12 (inset)

Printed in the United States of America at Corporate Graphics, in North Mankato, Minnesota.
6-2014
10 9 8 7 6 5 4 3 2 1

Table of Contents

How Do We Hear?

We use our ears to hear.

How does hearing work?

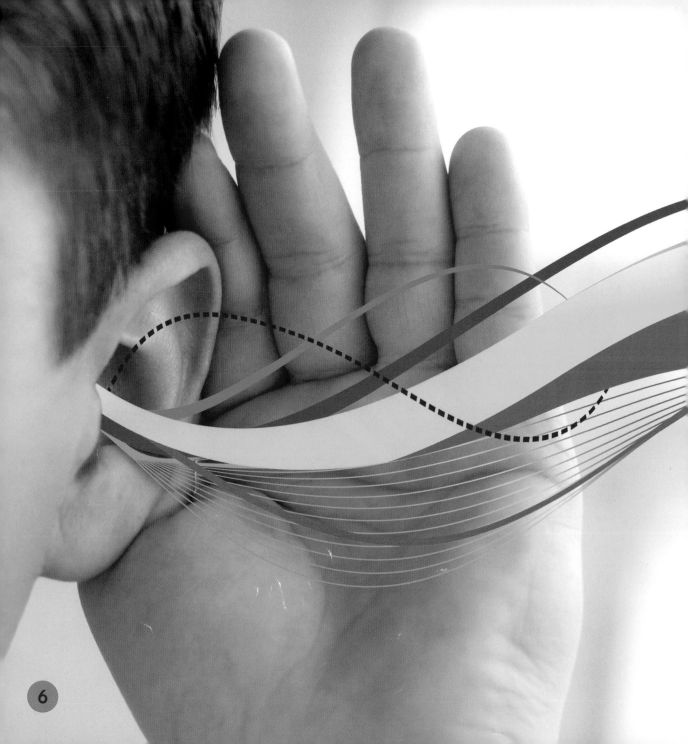

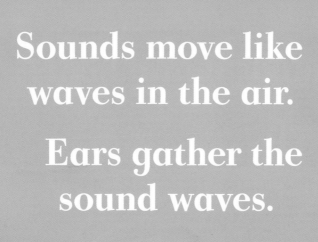

Sounds move like
waves in the air.

Ears gather the
sound waves.

The brain understands
the waves as sound.

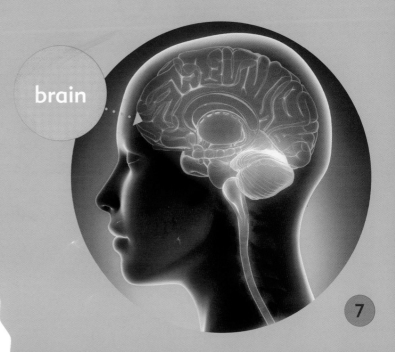

brain

What sounds do we hear? Beep! Beep!

alarm clock

Anne hears the alarm clock.
She knows it is time to get up.

9

Ding!
Lily hears the timer.
She knows the cookies are ready.

timer

11

Woof!

Axel hears his dog.

He knows she needs
to go out.

Honk!

Eddie hears the car horn.

He knows his ride is here.

Ring! Ring!
Mia hears the bell.

school
bell

She knows school is starting.

Max has trouble hearing.
He wears a hearing aid.
Now he can hear
the teacher better.

hearing
aid

What sounds do you hear?

What do they tell you?

Parts of the Ear

outer ear
The part of the ear that gathers sound waves.

middle ear
A part of the ear next to the ear canal; three bones move inside this air-filled part.

nerves
These small tubes send messages to the brain.

ear canal
A tube that carries sound into the ear.

eardrum
A round part inside the ear that moves back and forth when sound hits it.

inner ear
A part of the ear inside the head; fluid fills the inner ear.

Picture Glossary

alarm clock
A clock that
makes a sound
to wake you up.

hearing aid
A small machine
worn in or behind
the ear that makes
sound louder.

brain
A body part in
your head that
helps you think
and understand.

sound wave
A back and
forth movement
in the air that
carries noises.

Index

To Learn More

Learning more is as easy as 1, 2, 3.

1) Go to www.factsurfer.com

2) Enter "hearing" into the search box.

3) Click the "Surf" button to see a list of websites.

With factsurfer.com, finding more information is just a click away.

24